Results in Brief

Evaluation of Military Criminal Investigative Organizations' Child Sexual Assault Investigations

September 9, 2014

Objective

We evaluated 163 Military Criminal Investigative Organization (MCIO) investigations of sexual assaults of children closed in 2012 to determine whether the MCIOs completed investigations as required by DoD, Military Service, and MCIO guidance. Our evaluation focused on:

- whether the MCIOs investigated child sexual assaults as required by guiding policies and procedures.

Findings

- A total of 153 of 163 MCIO investigations (94 percent) met investigative standards.

- A total of 10 of 163 MCIO investigations (6 percent) had significant deficiencies. We returned those 10 cases to the MCIOs for follow-up corrective action.

- A total of 57 of the 163 cases had no investigative deficiencies.

- The remaining 96 cases had minor deficiencies that had no impact on the outcome or resolution of the investigation.

- All three MCIOs had instances in which:

  - they either did not issue or did not properly document the issuance of the DD Form 2701, "Initial Information for Victims and Witnesses of Crime," to victims or the appropriate guardian or family member;

  - subject, victim, and witness interviews were not thorough;

Findings Continued

  - logical investigative leads, such as interviews of witnesses, or leads gleaned during interviews were not addressed or conducted; and

  - physical or digital evidence was not collected.

Recommendations

- The Director and Commanders of the MCIOs:

  - continue to emphasize thorough completion of all child sexual assault investigations,

  - implement measures to improve the issuing and/or recording the DD Form 2701, and

  - consider enhancement of existing policy guidance regarding the collection of clothing and digital evidence

- The Director, Naval Criminal Investigative Service improve guidance and enhance supervision regarding responses to crime scenes.

Management Comments and Our Response

Management comments were generally responsive; however, the Commander, U.S. Army Criminal Investigation Command (CID) expressed concern regarding our review processes. The project's evaluation and reporting processes were independently evaluated and were found to comply with the Council of Inspectors General for Integrity and Efficiency (CIGIE) standards. We considered management comments on a draft of this report when preparing the final report and made changes as appropriate.

Recommendations Table

Management	No Additional Comments Required
The Director and Commanders of the Military Criminal Investigative Organizations	1, 2, 3, and 4.a
The Commander, U.S. Army Criminal Investigation Command	4.b
The Director, Naval Criminal Investigative Service	4.b and 5
The Commander, Air Force Office of Special Investigations	4.c

INSPECTOR GENERAL
DEPARTMENT OF DEFENSE
4800 MARK CENTER DRIVE
ALEXANDRIA, VIRGINIA 22350-1500

September 9, 2014

MEMORANDUM FOR COMMANDER, U.S. ARMY CRIMINAL INVESTIGATION COMMAND
DIRECTOR, NAVAL CRIMINAL INVESTIGATIVE SERVICE
COMMANDER, U.S. AIR FORCE OFFICE OF SPECIAL INVESTIGATIONS

SUBJECT: Evaluation of Military Criminal Investigative Organizations Child Sexual Assault Investigations (DODIG-2014-105)

This report is provided for review. We evaluated Military Criminal Investigative Organization (MCIOs') child sexual assault investigations to determine whether they achieved DoD, Military Service, and MCIO investigative standards. This was a self-initiated project to meet our statutory obligation to provide policy, oversight, and performance evaluation of all DoD activities relating to criminal investigation programs.

We determined that nearly all (94 percent) of the MCIOs' child sexual assault investigations evaluated met investigative standards or had only minor deficiencies. We returned cases with significant deficiencies to the responsible MCIOs for corrective action. Significant deficiencies are key evidence not being collected, crime scenes not examined, and witness or subject interviews not conducted or not thorough. The recommendations and findings outlined in this report are based on our analysis of the deficiencies identified during the case evaluations. We commend the MCIOs for their high compliance rate and determined approach to solving such heinous crimes against children.

Additionally, we invite your attention to Appendix B, "Case Details," which provides factual data on a myriad of child sexual assault characteristics. This information may prove helpful in combatting child sexual assault in the Department of Defense.

We considered management comments on a draft of this report when preparing the final report and made changes as appropriate. We appreciate the courtesies extended to the evaluation staff during the project. For more information on this report, please contact Mr. Chris Redmond at (703) 604-8556 (DSN 664-8556).

Randolph R. Stone
Deputy Inspector General
Policy and Oversight

Contents

Contents (cont'd)

Contents (cont'd)

Introduction

Objective

We evaluated 163 Military Criminal Investigative Organization (MCIO)[1] investigations of sexual assaults of children closed in 2012, to determine whether the MCIOs completed investigations as required by DoD, Military Service, and MCIO guidance. Our evaluation focused on:

- whether the MCIOs investigated child sexual assaults as required by guiding policies and procedures.

Background

The DoD Inspector General (IG) has statutory authority in accordance with the Inspector General Act of 1978, as amended, for policy, oversight, and performance evaluation with respect to all DoD activities relating to criminal investigation programs. This authority is embodied in DoD Directive (DoDD) 5106.01, "Inspector General of the Department of Defense (IG DoD)," April 20, 2012, and DoD Instruction (DoDI) 5505.03, "Initiation of Investigations by Defense Criminal Investigative Organizations," March 24, 2011.

Although many elements of a child sexual assault investigation are the same as any criminal investigation, child sexual assault investigations require unique skills gained through specialized training, especially in the approach taken to obtaining information from traumatized victims.

Within DoD, the MCIOs are responsible for investigating child sexual assaults.[2] Additionally, the MCIOs are responsible for developing specific investigative policy and requirements to govern the investigation of child sexual assault and for training assigned special agents in accordance with the Services' training standards. Service-specific policies emphasize the use of multidisciplinary teams to investigate and resolve child sexual abuse allegations. DoD and Service Family Advocacy Program (FAP) policies prescribe structure, participation, and

---

[1] The MCIOs include the U.S. Army Criminal Investigation Command, Naval Criminal Investigative Service, and Air Force Office of Special Investigations.

[2] Article 120b was added to the 2012 edition of the Uniform Code of Military Justice. The new article is designed to address only child sexual offenses and applies to child sexual assault offenses committed on or after June 28, 2012. Articles 120 and 125 (2008 edition) of the Uniform Code of Military Justice addresses child sexual assault offenses committed prior to June 28, 2012.

responsibilities of multidisciplinary teams. DoDD 6400.1, "Family Advocacy Program (FAP)," August 23, 2004, refers to the multidisciplinary teams as case review committees and they are made up of:

> designated individuals working at the installation level, tasked with the evaluation and determination of abuse and/or neglect cases and the development and coordination of treatment and disposition recommendations.

The DoD IG initiated this project to determine whether MCIO child sexual assault investigations were investigated in compliance with policy and guidance.

DoD Policy and Requirements

DoDD 6400.1 specifies it is DoD policy to:

> Prevent child abuse and domestic abuse involving persons... through public awareness, education, and family support programs provided by the FAP, and through standardized FAP programs and activities for military families who have been identified as at-risk of committing child abuse or domestic abuse.

> Promote early identification and coordinated, comprehensive intervention, assessment, and support to persons... who are victims of suspected child abuse or domestic abuse...

> Provide appropriate resource and referral information to persons... who are victims of alleged child abuse or domestic abuse.

DoDI 6400.3, "Family Advocacy Command Assistance Team," February 3, 1989, edition[3] defined child sexual abuse as:

> A category of abusive behavior within the definition of child abuse that includes the rape, molestation, prostitution, or other such form of sexual exploitation of a child; or incest with a child; or the employment, use, persuasion, inducement, enticement, or coercion of a child to engage in, or assist in, any sexually explicit conduct (or any simulation of such conduct).

---

[3] DoDI 6400.3 was reissued as DoDI 6400.03 on April 25, 2014. The 1989 edition of the DoDI was in effect during the course of the investigations that we evaluated.

Findings

Nearly all Child Sexual Assault Investigations Were Completed as Required by Guiding Policies

A total of 153 of 163 (94 percent) MCIO investigations met investigative standards or had only minor deficiencies. We also determined that MCIO child sexual assault investigative procedures largely complied with DoD and Military Service guidelines. However, we identified a few areas that need improvement.

In addition to analyzing the cases for compliance with guiding policies, we gleaned demographic and other case data.

Results of Child Sexual Assault Investigations

A total of 153 of 163 (94 percent) MCIO investigations met investigative standards or had only minor deficiencies. Fifty-seven cases (35 percent) met investigative standards because they had no deficiencies. In 96 cases (59 percent), we found only minor deficiencies that did not have a negative impact on the investigation. A total of 10 of 163 (6 percent) MCIO investigations had significant deficiencies. We returned the cases with significant deficiencies to the MCIOs for resolution. The MCIOs reopened 8 of the 10 cases for additional investigative work. For the remaining two cases, the MCIOs determined, and we agreed, additional investigative activity was not practicable due to the amount of time elapsed or based on their judgment that additional efforts would be futile. The DoD IG will oversee the results of reopened investigations.

Cases with No Deficiencies or Minor Deficiencies

Of the 163 cases evaluated, 153 (94 percent) either had no deficiencies or the deficiencies noted did not have a negative impact on the investigation. A total of 57 cases had no investigative deficiencies. The remaining 96 cases had 1 or more minor deficiencies that did not adversely affect the successful resolution of the investigation. Table 1 depicts a breakdown by MCIO of the number of cases, with no deficiencies or only minor deficiencies.

Table 1. Cases with No Deficiencies or Minor Deficiencies

Case Deficiency	Total	CID	NCIS	AFOSI
None	**57**	39	13	5
Minor Deficiencies	**96**	34	38	24
Total	**153**	**73**	**51**	**29**

See Appendix B for details of all sample results.

A "minor deficiency" is a task or investigative step the MCIO investigator did not perform, or performed not in conformity with DoD, Service, and MCIO policies and procedures. A minor deficiency is not likely to affect the outcome or have a negative impact on the investigation.

Examples of minor deficiencies[4] include, but are not limited to the following:

- delays in completing certain logical investigative steps,

- appropriate medical records were not collected and reviewed,

- victim (or parent or guardian) was not issued a DD Form 2701, "Initial Information for Victims and Witnesses of Crime,"

- routine briefs to the victim (or parent or guardian) about the status of the investigation were not provided, and

- record fingerprint impressions, mug photographs, and sample deoxyribonucleic acid (DNA) of subjects were not obtained.

Cases with Significant Deficiencies

Of the 163 cases evaluated, 10 cases (6 percent) had significant deficiencies. Table 2 depicts a breakdown by MCIO of the number of cases with significant deficiencies that were returned for possible correction.

Table 2. Cases with Significant Deficiencies

Cases	Total	CID	NCIS	AFOSI
Returned	**10**	6	3	1
Reopened	**8**	4	3	1

---

[4] The severity of the deficiencies depends in large part on the totality of the circumstances. What might be a minor deficiency in one investigation could very well be a significant deficiency in another.

A "significant deficiency" is one or more deficiencies resulting from a material failure(s) to conform to critical elements of DoD, Service, and MCIO policies and procedures. A significant deficiency indicates a breakdown in practices, programs, and/or policies having actual notable adverse impact on, or had a likelihood of materially affecting, the integrity of the investigation and/or adversely affecting or having a high probability of adversely affecting the outcome of an investigation. If our evaluation identified one or more significant deficiencies within an investigation, that investigation was returned to the relevant MCIO with an explanation of the deficiency(ies) as well as the supporting guidance and/or policy(ies) not followed.

Examples of significant deficiencies include, but are not limited to the following:

- key evidence was not collected from the crime scene, the victim, or the subject;

- crime scene examinations were not completed, not completed thoroughly, or not completed before the loss of crucial evidence;

- sexual assault forensic examinations were not conducted;

- witness interviews were not thorough or not conducted; and

- subject and victim interviews or re-interviews were not thorough or not conducted.

We provided information on the 10 investigations with significant deficiencies to the respective MCIOs. We asked the MCIOs to consider our findings and, where practicable, reopen those cases to conduct additional investigative activity to address deficiencies. In some instances, reopening the investigation would not be a prudent use of investigative resources due to the length of time elapsed or judgment that additional efforts would be futile.

Cases Returned to CID

We returned six cases to CID for consideration of our findings. On August 8, 2013, CID agreed to reopen four of the six cases to conduct additional activity. CID declined to pursue additional investigative activity for the two remaining cases because they believed it would not alter the outcome of the case or too much time had elapsed, causing the recommended investigative activity to be impracticable. We agreed with CID's assessment of the two remaining cases.

Cases Returned to NCIS

We returned three cases to NCIS for consideration of our findings. On September 26, 2013, NCIS agreed to reopen the returned cases to conduct additional activity.

Cases Returned to AFOSI

We returned one case to AFOSI for consideration of our findings. On July 11, 2013, AFOSI agreed to reopen the returned case to conduct additional activity.

Analysis of Investigative Deficiencies

We analyzed the combined data related to both minor and significant deficiencies found in a total of 106 cases (96 with minor and 10 with significant deficiencies) to identify and assess patterns and trends and make recommendations to improve investigative quality. Our analysis disclosed five categories of deficiencies including: 1) interview and post-interview, 2) evidence, 3) crime scene documentation and/or processing, 4) subject-focused actions, and 5) investigative coordination and administrative deficiencies.

Interview and Post-Interview Deficiencies

In total, 78 of the 163 sample cases had interview and post-interview deficiencies. We categorized them by subject, victim, and witness interview and post-interview deficiencies to more efficiently analyze the results. Table 3 depicts a breakdown by MCIO of the number of cases with interview deficiencies.

Table 3. Cases with Interview and Post-Interview Deficiencies

Total	CID	NCIS	AFOSI
78	26	34	18

Subject Interview and Post-Interview Deficiencies

We found two areas affecting all three MCIOs related to the thoroughness of subject interviews and post-interview actions, which when separated by MCIO, are not indicative of patterns and trends; however are noteworthy: 1) Some subject interviews were not thorough[5] and did not address all of the elements of the

---

[5] For this evaluation project, thoroughness is defined as obtaining basic facts and relevant information, to include elements of the offense or pertinent information surrounding the matter being investigated, and identifying and following pertinent investigative leads.

offense, and 2) investigators did not follow up on all logical leads stemming from interviews. Table 4 depicts a breakdown by MCIO of the number of cases with subject interview deficiencies.

Table 4. Subject Interview and Post-Interview Deficiencies

Area of Concern	Total	CID	NCIS	AFOSI
Subject interview was not thorough and did not address all the elements of the offense.	**10**	2	4	4
Investigators did not follow up on logical leads stemming from interviews.	**8**	1	3	4

Victim Interview and Post-Interview Deficiencies

We separated victim interview and post-interview deficiencies into three areas of concern: 1) the interview was not thorough, considering the circumstances of the case and age of the victim, because pertinent information surrounding the assault was omitted and could have been obtained by investigators, 2) logical leads stemming from interviews were not developed or pursued, and 3) investigators did not issue or document that they issued a DD Form 2701 to the victims or their guardians. Additionally, we found 11 instances where NCIS investigators either did not brief the victims or their guardians on the status and various aspects of the investigations, or did not document that the briefs were conducted. We found only one instance where CID either did not brief a victim as required, or did not document the briefing in the case file. Unlike CID and NCIS, victim or guardian briefings is not a policy requirement for AFOSI investigations. Table 5 depicts a breakdown by MCIO of the number of cases with the identified deficiencies.

Table 5. Victim Interview and Post-Interview Deficiencies

Area of Concern	Total	CID	NCIS	AFOSI
Victim interview was not thorough	**11**	3	5	3
Logical leads stemming from interview were not developed or pursued.	**10**	4	2	4
Victim or victim's guardian was not issued a DD Form 2701 (or the issuance was not documented as required).	**36**	18	11	7

Witness Interview and Post-Interview Deficiencies

We separated witness interview and post-interview action deficiencies into two areas of concern: 1) witnesses were identified but not interviewed, and the file contained no documented explanation for why they were not interviewed and 2) canvass interviews[6] were not conducted when appropriate.[7] Table 6 depicts a breakdown by MCIO of the number of cases with the identified deficiencies.

Table 6. Witness Interview and Post-Interview Deficiencies

Area of Concern	Total	CID	NCIS	AFOSI
Witnesses were identified but not interviewed, and the file was not documented to explain why.	**37**	7	21	9
Canvass interviews were not conducted.	**17**	4	10	3

For the most part, these deficiencies were minor and did not adversely impact the outcome of the investigation. Only eight instances (CID 4; NCIS 3; AFOSI 1) were found in cases considered to be significantly deficient. Investigative thoroughness demands pertinent investigative leads be followed. Absent some explanation of why certain leads were not completed, i.e., perhaps related to most efficient use of investigative resources that management and supporting legal counsel deemed unnecessary (as they would result in cumulative unneeded evidence), case-reviewers are left to ponder why investigators did not interview certain witnesses.

Additionally, we identified two witness-interviews with thoroughness deficiencies. Although interview thoroughness could have an adverse effect on a case, our evaluation indicates these two to be anomalous and not systemic deficiencies.

Evidence Deficiencies

Of the total cases (163) evaluated, there were 25 (15 percent) with evidence deficiencies. We found 11 percent of CID's cases (9 of 79), 19 percent of NCIS' cases (10 of 54), and 20 percent of AFOSI's cases (6 of 20) with evidence deficiencies. The deficiencies included not collecting all items of physical evidence (for example, clothing, bed linens, phone records, text message records) identified by subjects, victims, or witnesses. The only item we consider to represent a pattern or trend relates to the collection, and search of digital evidence identified by the subject(s),

---

[6] Canvass interviews are interviews conducted in the immediate vicinity of a crime scene in an effort to identify witnesses or information related to the matter being investigated.

[7] See Appendix B for additional information on the areas of concern.

suspect(s), victim(s), or witnesses during investigations that could have had evidentiary value. This evidence was not collected in several instances by all three MCIOs. Evidence deficiencies are never desirable; however, we consider the remaining deficiencies to be anomalous and not indicative of patterns or trends and the information is provided for transparency and MCIO action deemed appropriate. Table 7 depicts a breakdown by MCIO of the 31 evidence deficiencies among the 25 cases.

Table 7. Evidence Deficiencies

Investigators did not:	Total	CID	NCIS	AFOSI
Collect all items of clothing and bed linen evidence identified by subject(s), victim(s), or witness(es).	**4**	1	3	0
Collect sexual assault forensic examination evidence of subject(s) or victim(s).	**3**	1	0	2
Collect appropriate digital evidence identified by subject(s), victim(s), or witness(es).	**13**	5	5	3
Collect appropriate DNA sample from subject(s), suspect(s), victim(s), and witness(es) for evidence comparison.	**5**	1	3	1
Submit appropriate computer and/or cell phone to laboratory for examination.	**6**	1	3	2

Note: The disparity in the number of cases with evidence deficiencies and the total number of deficiencies is due to some cases having multiple deficiencies.

Of the 163 investigations, 19 (12 percent) contained evidence collection deficiencies. Among those 19 investigations, 4 investigations (CID 1 and NCIS 3) involved investigators not collecting the victim's, subject's, or suspect's clothing and/or bed linen as recommended by MCIO policies. In 3 of the 4 cases that clothing and/or bed linen was not obtained, the MCIO (CID 1 and NCIS 2) was notified within 5 days of the assault. In the fourth instance, 10 days had elapsed before NCIS was notified of the assault. Interestingly, CID with one deficiency, is the only MCIO that mandates the collection of clothing worn by the victim or subject, whereas, NCIS and AFOSI policies provide investigators some discretion regarding the collection of subject's and victim's clothing. For AFOSI, this appears to be working well as we noted no deficiencies in this category.

As previously mentioned, all three MCIOs had digital evidence collection deficiencies. Additionally, we noted six cases in which agents did not submit computers and/or cell phones they collected as evidence to the laboratory for examination. This amounts to a total of 19 investigations with digital evidence deficiencies. There is no overarching DoD or Military Service policy guidance related to digital evidence collection. MCIO policies for digital evidence collection varied. CID policy mandates the preservation and collection of digital evidence during the course of criminal investigations. NCIS policy highlights agents should consider computers and their related peripherals and media at crime scenes as potential evidence. AFOSI policy contains a comprehensive list of digital evidence to consider seizing in child sexual assault investigations.

Crime Scene Documentation and/or Processing Deficiencies

In total, 33 cases (20 percent) had crime scene documentation and/or processing deficiencies. We separated the crime scene documentation and/or processing deficiencies into two areas of concern: 1) crime scene examination or validation and 2) evidence collection at crime scenes. Crime scene validations are less thorough examinations of a scene. These less thorough examinations may be appropriate in an investigation when there is a delay in reporting to law enforcement and collection of physical evidence may no longer be possible. Validations normally consist of documenting observations, photographing, and preparing rough sketches. Validations are important because they provide valuable investigative information and assist during interviews. In addition, the documentation from validations helps others understand how events occurred. Table 8 depicts 30 of 36 total deficiencies broken down by MCIO of the crime scene documentation and/or processing deficiencies among the 33 cases.

Table 8. Crime Scene Documentation and/or Processing Deficiencies

Investigators did not:	Total	CID	NCIS	AFOSI
Examine or validate the crime scene.	**23**	6	11	6
Collect potential evidence from the scene.	**7**	3	2	2

Note: The disparity in the number of cases with crime scene documentation and/or processing deficiencies and the total number of deficiencies is due to some cases having multiple deficiencies. Table 8 represents 30 deficiencies in 33 cases.

The remaining six deficiencies relate to photographing a crime scene (2 deficiencies), sketching a crime scene (3 deficiencies), and having documented authority to search a crime scene (1 deficiency). Although these crime scene deficiencies could have an adverse effect on a case, our evaluation indicates these deficiencies to be anomalous and not a systemic issue.

Crime Scene Examination or Validation

As reflected in Table 8, investigators did not conduct crime scene examinations or validations in 23 cases. In 11 investigations, the sexual assault was reported within 4 days of the date of the incident and a crime scene should have been available; however, the investigators did not conduct a crime scene examination and did not attempt to collect physical evidence from the scene. In the remaining 12 cases, investigators could have responded to the scene(s) to validate them by documenting observations, photographing the scene, and preparing sketches.

Only six CID investigations (8 percent) lacked crime scene examinations or validations. CID policy requires agents to promptly examine a crime scene when available in any CID investigation. Other than the six, documentation indicates CID agents consistently completed crime scene examinations, thoroughly completed documentation, and routinely included detailed observations, photographs, and sketches.

A total of 11 NCIS investigations (20 percent) lacked a crime scene examination or validation. NCIS policy regarding crime scene processing for sexual assault cases uses the word "should" throughout its policy which is neither mandatory nor directive in nature. As such, the lack of crime scene examinations or validations did not violate NCIS policy.

A total of 6 AFOSI investigations (20 percent) lacked a crime scene examination or validation. During the timeframe in which cases included in the scope of this evaluation were investigated, AFOSI did not have policy guidance that required crime scene examinations. AFOSI agents relied on training and AFOSI Manual (AFOSIMAN) 71-124, "Crime Scene Manual," September 30, 2003, regarding crime scene processing and evidence collection. AFOSIMAN 71-124 is a "how-to" manual regarding searches, seizures, and evidence collection procedures, which was not regulatory in nature and does not specify when to conduct crime scene examinations or validations. However, subsequent to the start of this evaluation, AFOSI reissued AFOSIMAN 71-122, volume 1, "Criminal Investigations," on March 1, 2013, which directs "...all crime scenes are located and documented (photographed/sketched)...." At the time these cases were investigated, the processing and collection of crime scene evidence did not violate AFOSI policies.

Subject-Focused Action and Investigative Coordination Administrative Deficiencies

We also noted some minor deviations from MCIO policy guidance that appear to be anomalous in the areas of "subject-focused action deficiencies" related to the improper release of subject(s)/suspect(s) to unit personnel, and the conduct of criminal history checks on subject(s). Additionally, we noted some cases with minor MCIO policy shortcomings in the areas of investigative coordination with forensic science coordinators and documentation of supervisory reviews. See Appendix B for details.

Demographic and Other Case Data

In addition to analyzing the cases for compliance with guiding policies, we gleaned information related to various topics including alcohol use by the subject and victim; age ranges; pay grades of subjects; where the offenses occurred; the relationship, if any, between the subject and victim; the number and type of primary offenses investigated; cases with multiple subjects and victims; and disciplinary action, if any. We did not draw conclusions concerning the data. The data are provided for information only and for possible future analysis if compared to data gleaned from comparable statistical samples. See Appendix B for details.

The primary offenses that occurred were rape of a child, aggravated sexual assault of a child, aggravated sexual abuse of a child, aggravated sexual contact with a child, abusive sexual contact with a child, and indecent liberties with a child.

The offenses occurred both on and off military installations, in a variety of settings, such as family residences, daycare centers, hotels, and parks. In some instances, the exact location where the offense occurred could not be determined.

We observed and documented the types of relationships between the subject and the victim, to include determining the subject's or the victim's military affiliation. We also analyzed a host of other victim- and subject-specific data such as age, pay grade, and gender.

We also collected and analyzed the disciplinary action taken against the subjects of the investigations. Disciplinary actions taken against the subjects included court-martial, punitive discharge, administrative separations, civilian prosecution, non-judicial punishment, reprimand, counseling, other actions, and no action taken. See Appendix B, Tables B.30 to B.34, for details. We did not analyze whether the action was appropriate. The propriety or appropriateness of disciplinary actions taken by commanders, based on legal guidance, was not within the scope of this evaluation.

Conclusions

A total of 153 of 163 (94 percent) MCIO investigations met investigative standards, or had only minor deficiencies. A total of 57 of 163 cases (35 percent) had no deficiencies, and 96 of 163 cases (59 percent) had only minor deficiencies.

A total of 10 of 163 cases (6 percent) had significant deficiencies including:

- key evidence was not collected from the crime scene, the victim, or the subject;

- crime scene examinations were not completed, not completed thoroughly, or not completed before the loss of crucial evidence;

- victim was not medically examined;

- witness interviews were not thorough or not conducted; and

- subject and victim interviews or reinterviews were not thorough or not conducted.

We returned the cases with significant deficiencies to the MCIOs for resolution.

Initial Information for Victims and Witnesses of Crime

Of the 163 cases evaluated, 36 lacked documentation that agents issued a DD Form 2701, "Initial Information for Victims and Witnesses of Crime," to the victims or to their appropriate family member or guardian. The DD Form 2701 provides victims and witnesses to a crime with an understanding of the military criminal justice process, actions to take in certain situations, a list of victim rights, and contact information if more assistance is needed. DoDI 1030.2, "Victim and Witness Assistance Procedures," June 4, 2004, requires not only the issuance of the form, but that the issuance be recorded as "evidence the officer notified the victim or witness of his or her statutory rights."

Interviews

In total, 100 of the 163 sample cases had interview and post-interview deficiencies. Improvement is needed in conducting and documenting thorough interviews of victims, suspects, subjects, and witnesses. A thorough interview enables investigators to corroborate or refute the information obtained as well as identify any logical investigative leads.

Collection of Evidence

We found several incidents where the MCIOs did not consistently collect digital evidence, as required by their policies, such as cell phones or computers with possible probative value that was identified by the victim(s), suspect(s), or subject(s) during interviews. CID policy on digital evidence is not specific to child sexual assault investigations, but does specify the preservation and collection of digital evidence during the course of criminal investigations. NCIS does not have policy that specifies the collection of digital evidence, but NCIS policy regarding evidence collection states, "physical evidence may be defined as articles or material found in an investigation which will assist in the solution of the crime and the prosecution of the criminal." NCIS is currently revising policy regarding the collection of digital evidence. AFOSI policy is specific to child sexual assault investigations, and contains a comprehensive list of digital media to consider collecting.

In all but four cases, the MCIOs identified and or collected the victim(s), suspect(s), or subject(s) clothing as required by their individual policies. CID policy mandates the collection of the subject's and victim's clothing worn during the assault, regardless of its probative value. NCIS policy states that clothing of the victims and suspects should be seized and processed as evidence. AFOSI policy directs investigators to collect the victim(s) and subject(s) clothing in sexual assault investigations. We acknowledge the MCIOs recent efforts to enhance their response to sexual assault in the Department. Subsequent to the start of this project, CID published CID Pamphlet 195-12, "Sex Assault Investigation Handbook," April 23, 2013, updating their requirement to collect clothing worn by the subjects or victims immediately after the assault. NCIS is currently revising policy regarding the collection of clothing worn by the victim, subject(s) or suspect(s). AFOSI also updated AFOSIMAN 71-124, 30 September 2003, Paragraphs 5.1.1.5. and 5.10.1., to further detail the requirement to collect clothing worn by the subject and victim.

Crime Scene Examinations

We found crime scene documentation and/or processing deficiencies in 33 of 163 cases. Neither DoD nor the Military Services have policy to establish MCIO crime scene documentation and/or processing requirements. As a result, the MCIOs have differing crime scene examination policies. CID policy guidance on crime scenes examinations is comprehensive and requires investigators to conduct crime scene examinations, sketches and photographs. NCIS policy is ambiguous; it neither requires an investigator to conduct a crime scene examination nor complete a sketch, but does require photographs. AFOSI policy, at the time these cases were investigated, did not require investigators to conduct crime scene examinations, sketches, or photographs. However, as of March 1, 2013, subsequent to the start of this project, AFOSI reissued AFOSIMAN 71-122, volume 1, which now directs all crime scenes be located and documented (photographed and/or sketched). With the exception of six cases, CID agents documented and processed crime scenes as required by their guiding policies. Both NCIS and AFOSI had a number of cases wherein, they did not document or process crime scenes. Their policies at the time either did not establish requirements, or provided for some agent discretion. Therefore, neither NCIS nor AFOSI violated their policies for processing or documenting crime scene examinations at the time of this project.

Management Comments on the Report and Our Response

CID Comments

CID challenged the accuracy and presentation of certain report information especially the comingling of minor and significant deficiencies; however, the CID Commander ultimately commented that CID is ready and willing to assist the DoD IG in efforts to improve the quality of criminal investigations. CID remains committed to ensuring the best possible support to the Army soldiers, civilians, and families.

NCIS Comments

NCIS is currently updating policy and training to include child sexual assault in its Advanced Family and Sexual Violence Training Program (AFSVTP), during which investigators receive training from nationally recognized and DoD subject matter experts. In response to this report, and evolving requirements identified within the DoD Special Victim Capability program, NCIS will conduct a curriculum review for the AFSVTP and include the recommendations from this report in future AFSVTP courses and training.

AFOSI Comments

AFOSI is committed to developing and providing high-quality policy and training to its special agents to ensure field units have the capability to conduct professional investigations. AFOSI expressed appreciation for the value this assessment serves in fostering discussions and necessary actions geared to maintain and improve MCIO criminal investigators' knowledge and skills.

Our Response

In response to the concerns expressed by CID, our Office of Audit Policy and Oversight reviewed this final report and associated evidence for factual data accuracy, fairness and objectivity for compliance with the CIGIE Inspection and Evaluation reporting standard (See Appendix E for details). IPO made appropriate report updates to ensure data accuracy, relevance, and objectivity.

We further acknowledge the concern expressed by the CID Commander regarding the reporting of minor and significant deficiencies; however, we analyzed both to identify patterns and trends to make recommendations that will result in improved investigative quality. We value the MCIOs' cooperation during this evaluation and commend their efforts to improve child sexual assault investigations. We further applaud the initiatives enacted by the NCIS and the AFOSI during this evaluation to update training and policy to further enhance investigations of child sexual assault.

Recommendations, MCIO Comments, and Our Response

Recommendation 1. Adequacy of Investigations

We recommend that the Director and Commanders of the Military Criminal Investigative Organizations continue to emphasize thorough completion of all child sexual assault investigations to ensure all investigations are completed as required by DoD, Service, and command regulatory guidance.

CID Comments

The Commander, CID stated they "continue to" emphasize thorough investigations, as "indicative of this MCIO's 92 percent compliance rate."

NCIS Comments

The Director of NCIS agreed and stated that it will continue to emphasize thorough completion of all child sexual assault investigations as required by DoD, Service, and NCIS regulatory guidance.

AFOSI Comments

AFOSI agreed and stated that AFOSI is committed to providing high-quality investigative products to Air Force decision makers and will re-emphasize to its field personnel and staff personnel at the USAF Special Investigations Academy (USAFSIA) during training the importance of conducting thorough, complete investigations.

Our Response

After assessing CID's comments, we revised our recommendation to include "continue to" in the recommendation.

The comments are responsive. We recognize and applaud the MCIOs' commitment to timely and thorough child sexual assault investigations. It is clear the MCIOs understand the impact that the quality of their child sexual assault investigations has on the Department. No further comments are required."

Recommendation 2. Issuance of the DD Form 2701

We recommend that the Director and Commanders of the Military Criminal Investigative Organizations implement measures to improve issuing and/or recording the issuance of the DD Form 2701 to victims or their appropriate family member or guardian.

CID Comments

The Commander of CID disagreed with the recommendation. CID commented that we incorrectly assessed the findings, as we could not specify in our report that the DD Forms 2701 were not issued, only that the issuance was not documented in the case file. The Commander CID recommended we change the recommendation to, implement measures to either improve the issuing of the DD Form 2701 or the documentation of such issuances in case files.

NCIS Comments

NCIS agreed and stated NCIS is currently revising policy regarding child sexual assault investigations. Included in the revision is specific guidance for the delivery of the DD Form 270I to appropriate family members or guardians of child victims.

AFOSI Comments

AFOSI agreed and asserted that only 11 cases had DD Form 2701 deficiencies, and of those 11 cases, a few were attributable to local law enforcement officials interfacing with the respective victim, family member, or guardian, and not AFOSI personnel.

Our Response

After assessing CID's comments, we revised our recommendation to comport to CID's suggestion and included "improve issuing and/or recording the issuance of the DD Form 2701 to victims or their appropriate family member or guardian." As a result of AFOSI comments, we revised our Finding.

The comments are responsive. We recognize NCIS' efforts to revise current policy to include specific guidance on issuing the DD Form 2701. No further comments are required.

Recommendation 3. Interviews

We recommended that the Director and Commanders of the Military Criminal Investigative Organizations continue to place increased emphasis on interview thoroughness, to include the pursuit of logical leads identified during the interview, through continued training, supervision, and policy improvements.

CID Comments

CID agreed with the recommendation. CID commented that the thoroughness of interviews will continue to be emphasized within their organization, highlighting that less than seven percent of all significant and minor deficiencies identified in the report were thoroughness deficiencies.

NCIS Comments

NCIS agreed and stated that NCIS will continue to emphasize interview thoroughness and the pursuit of logical leads.

AFOSI Comments

AFOSI agreed and stated that in two of the five instances involving interviews as not thorough, it was not AFOSI investigators that conducted those interviews, but investigators from another agency. Headquarters AFOSI staff assessed two other interviews deemed to be not thorough in our report and determined those interviews were thoroughly conducted. AFOSI also expressed concern that we evaluated child sexual assault victim interviews with the same set of parameters as those for adult sexual assault interviews.

Additionally, AFOSI has increased training and the use of the Cognitive Interview technique during basic and advanced training. Further, AFOSI agreed that victim interviews and probative investigative activities conducted by investigators are important.

Our Response

The comments are responsive. We acknowledge AFOSI's efforts to increase the use of the Cognitive Interview technique during basic and advanced agent training. We also acknowledge AFOSI agents were not solely responsible for some of the interviews referenced as "not thorough" in the referenced cases as they were investigated jointly with another agency and we have corrected our report.

Regarding the two interviews judged by AFOSI as "thorough" that we assessed to be "not thorough," we reexamined the details of those two cases. In one case, the interview was assessed as not thorough as the recorded interview of the victim demonstrated the victim was of an appropriate age to articulate relevant facts, was mature, and fully engaged during the interview, but was not asked pertinent questions. In the remaining case, the victim was not asked about the clothing worn during the assault. It is clear the MCIOs recognize the importance of child interviews as highlighted by their high compliance rate in this category. No further comments are required.

Recommendation 4. Collection of Evidence

a. We recommended that the Director and Commanders of the Military Criminal Investigative Organizations enhance guidance and increase training to highlight the critical role that clothing and digital evidence has in child sexual assault investigations and subsequent prosecutions.

CID Comments

CID agreed but contended that our evaluation did not identify errors related to digital evidence collection.

NCIS Comments

NCIS agreed. NCIS is currently revising policy regarding child sexual assault investigations and evidence collection procedures to include the identification and collection of clothing, and digital, electronic, and storage evidence.

AFOSI Comments

AFOSI agreed. However, AFOSI commented that in some cases with deficiencies pertaining to collection of digital evidence, it was either the responsibility of another law enforcement agency or there was nothing in the facts or circumstances indicating there was evidence on the devices; and therefore, no supporting legal basis for obtaining the necessary search authority to seize the item(s). Moreover, AFOSI commented that our assessment, which emphasizes the use of protocols, did not allow for field judgments and it is not reasonable or practical to seize all items of evidence for laboratory analysis. AFOSI stated that AFOSI forensic specialists work with case agents to access the probative value of evidence on a case-by-case basis.

Our Response

The comments are responsive. We disagree with CID's contention that our evaluation did not identify errors related to digital evidence collection. Our evaluation found digital evidence collection errors in five CID investigations that were identified and reported in the draft report CID received (Table 7). We appreciate the efforts by CID and NCIS to evaluate and enhance their existing policy in this area. With regard to the investigations referenced by AFOSI as lacking a legal basis for a search warrant, the evaluation of those investigations were void of documented efforts relating to requesting consent searches. Pursuing consent searches is a viable alternative to search authorizations and could have been explored in the referenced investigations. Further, AFOSI's assertion that our assessment conveyed that AFOSI policy should embrace protocols that did not allow for field judgments and/or decisions and collect all items of evidence regardless of probative value is incorrect. Our report neither encourages nor discourages the use of protocols. Further, we do not discourage the use of field judgments nor do we advocate collecting all evidence regardless of probative value. Our assessments and recommendations are tailored to each investigation based on the facts detailed in the documents provided for the project. No further comments are required.

> **b. We recommend the Commander, United States Army Criminal Investigation Command, and the Director, Naval Criminal Investigative Service, evaluate existing policies and enhance their guidance regarding the collection of digital evidence including computers and other electronic media used by the subject(s), suspect(s), and when applicable, victim(s).**

CID Comments

CID agreed but contended that our evaluation did not identify errors related to digital evidence collection.

NCIS Comments

NCIS agreed and is currently revising policy regarding child sexual assault investigations and evidence collection procedures to include the identification and collection of clothing, and digital, electronic, and storage evidence.

Our Response

CID and NCIS comments are responsive. We disagree with CID's contention that our evaluation did not identify errors related to digital evidence collection. Our evaluation found digital evidence collection errors in five CID investigations, which we highlighted in an earlier response to CID's comments. We appreciate the efforts by CID and NCIS to enhance their existing policies in this area. No further comments are required.

c. We recommend the Commander, Air Force Office of Special Investigations; implement measures to improve compliance with existing policies regarding the collection of computers and other digital media.

AFOSI Comments

AFOSI agreed. AFOSI will summarize the concerns identified in our assessment and provide that information to USAFSIA to ensure appropriate emphasis during training on the importance of evidence recognition and collection. However, AFOSI questioned the basis for this recommendation pertaining only to AFOSI as AFOSI figures did not appear to be greatly different than those for CID and NCIS.

Our Response

AFOSI comments are responsive. This recommendation pertained only to AFOSI because we identified that although AFOSI has comprehensive policy on digital evidence, AFOSI did not always comply with that policy. In Recommendation 4.b, CID and NCIS were asked to evaluate their existing policies and enhance their guidance regarding the collection of digital evidence, as their policies were not as specific or as detailed as AFOSI's. We commend AFOSI's efforts to highlight the significance of child sexual assault investigations through staff emphasis and training at the USAFSIA. No further comments are required.

Recommendation 5. Crime Scene Validations

We recommend the Director, Naval Criminal Investigative Service improve guidance and enhance supervision regarding responses to crime scenes.

NCIS Comments

NCIS agreed and is revising policy to include specific guidance for the identification and collection of clothing, digital, and electronic storage evidence. The policy revisions will also include an emphasis on crime scene response.

Our Response

NCIS comments are responsive. No further comments are required.

Appendix A

Scope and Methodology

We conducted this evaluation from April 2013 through July 2013. Our work included an evaluation of child sexual assault investigations completed (closed and adjudicated) in 2012 for compliance with DoD, Military Service, and MCIO policy requirements effective at the time of the investigation while noting observations and deficiencies.

We conducted the evaluation in accordance with the professional standards for evaluation established by the Council of the Inspectors General for Integrity and Efficiency. We believe that the evidence obtained provides a reasonable basis for our observations and recommendations based on our objectives. We used professional judgment in making observations and recommendations.

We evaluated the MCIOs' child sexual assault investigative policy guidance to assess the extent to which it addressed investigative activity expected to be conducted in response to child sexual assault reports. We familiarized ourselves with tasks expected in any child sexual assault investigation.

Our unique vantage point in assessing child sexual assault investigations across the MCIOs permits us to identify both minor and significant deficiencies, and affords us the opportunity to not only identify Department wide patterns, trends, and best practices, but if applicable, provide the MCIOs with recommendations for improvement, and or action(s) the MCIOs regard as appropriate or relevant.

At the onset of the evaluation, we sent a data call memorandum to each MCIO requesting a listing of the sexual assault investigations with child victims which were closed (completed and adjudicated) in 2012. The listings provided by the MCIOs included the case numbers, dates the cases were opened and closed, the numbers of subjects and victims in each case, the criminal offense investigated, and the MCIO office where the investigation was conducted. The listings established the population for this project. We worked with the DoD OIG Quantitative Methods Division (QMD) to determine a simple random sample number of cases, stratified by MCIO, to evaluate based on a desired level of reliability giving us our sample size. The sample size was selected from the population using a 90-percent confidence level, 50-percent probability of occurrence at a 5-percent precision level. Our final total of cases to evaluate was 163 cases.

The project of child sexual assault investigation was based on offenses defined in the UCMJ 2008 and 2012 Editions, Articles 120 and 125 as listed in Tables A.1 through A.3. For this evaluation, a "child" is defined as a person younger than 16 years of age based on UCMJ victim age specifications for the applicable offenses. We also included the evaluation of investigations if applicable state laws defined a child as a person younger than 17 years of age.

Table A.1. Article 120b Child Sexual Assault Offenses – UCMJ 2012 Edition

Offense/Manual for Courts-Martial
Rape of a child under 12
Rape of a child over 12 but under 16
Sexual assault of a child under 16
Sexual abuse of a child under 16 (lewd act) (including any sexual contact with a child, indecent exposure to a child communicating indecent language to a child, and committing indecent conduct with or in the presence of a child)

Table A.2. Article 120 Child Sexual Assault Offenses – UCMJ 2008 Edition

Offense/Manual for Courts-Martial
Rape of a child (Article 120b)
Aggravated sexual assault of a child under 12 (Article 120d)
Aggravated sexual abuse of a child under 12 (Article 120f)
Aggravated sexual contact with a child under 16 (Article 120g)
Aggravated sexual assault of a child over 12 but under 16 (Article 120d)
Aggravated sexual abuse of a child under 16 (Article 120f)
Abusive sexual contact with a child under 16 (Article 120i)
Indecent liberties with a child under 16 (120j)

Table A.3. Article 125 Child Sexual Assault Offenses – UCMJ 2008 Edition

Offense/Manual for Courts-Martial
Sodomy of a child under 12 (Article 125a(2))
Sodomy of a child over 12 but under 16 (Article 125a(3))

We developed a child sexual assault case review protocol for each MCIO based on DoD, Military Service, and each MCIO's investigative policies and procedures. The protocol addressed, in detail, all investigative steps required to complete a thorough child sexual assault investigation ensuring compliance with applicable DoD, Military Service, and MCIO policies that were in effect during the life of the investigation.

In conducting the evaluation, we noted observations and deficiencies, both minor and significant, found in the investigative files using the following definitions:

Observations. Observations are aspects of an investigation that the case reviewer deemed warranted added attention and documentation. Observations may also be administrative errors in a report or specific information the MCIOs requested we look for during our case evaluations.

Minor Deficiency. A minor deficiency is a task or investigative step the MCIO did not perform, or performed not in conformity with DoD, Service, and MCIO policies and procedures. A minor deficiency is not likely to affect the outcome or have a negative impact on the investigation.

Significant Deficiency. An investigation will be found to contain significant deficiencies if one or more deficiencies result from a material failure(s) to conform with critical elements of DoD, Service, and MCIO policies and procedures. A significant deficiency indicates a breakdown in practices, programs, and/or policies having actual notable adverse impact on, or had a likelihood of materially affecting, the integrity of the investigation and/or adversely affecting or having a high probability of adversely affecting the outcome of an investigation. The procedure for documenting cases with significant deficiencies is addressed below.

Not all investigations with significant deficiencies warranted reopening. An example of an investigation that should be reopened would be an investigation that failed to fully identify and interview all potential victims. In this example, identifying and interviewing additional victims may lead to subsequent prosecution of an offender. The reopening of an investigation would not be expected or beneficial when the MCIO did not conduct time-critical investigative steps or failed to conduct them according to established policy. Examples include conducting telephonic subject and victim interviews or failing to collect crucial evidence from a crime scene. These investigative steps are time sensitive and the opportunity to complete these steps cannot be replicated during the course of reopening an investigation. Although not properly interviewing the victim and/or subject or collecting crucial evidence has a significant impact and/or adverse outcome of the investigation, reopening the investigation cannot overcome those errors.

At the conclusion of the case evaluation phase, the data collected and stored in the protocol database was analyzed through the use of numerous queries that were built to efficiently identify investigative tasks and steps that were not completed by some or all of the MCIOs. The queries showed what tasks or steps were involved with each deficiency and the number of instances of each.

Cases identified as containing possible significant deficiencies were documented in a detailed work paper which recorded all deficiencies and observations as identified by the evaluator. A peer review was completed wherein a second evaluator reviewed the investigation and documented concurrence or nonoccurrence with identified deficiencies. The Project Manager evaluated the deficiencies, the applicable guidance identified, and documented their assessment. Upon completion of the evaluator assessment, peer review, and Project Manager analysis, the work paper was reviewed by the Project Director who determined final resolution of the case file. If the case was determined to contain significant deficiencies, it was returned to the MCIO for review and resolution. Upon completion of all the work papers for a specific MCIO, a "Predraft Results Memo" was prepared that outlined the tentative results of the evaluation. The *Predraft Results Memo* identified the number of cases evaluated, number of cases identified with minor deficiencies, and those identified with significant deficiencies. The memorandum and all approved work papers were provided to the MCIO with a request to evaluate our assessment of the significantly deficient investigations and provide comment. We updated the protocol database to reflect the final outcome of the work paper when it was determined to contain only minor deficiencies and/or observations. We will evaluate subsequent investigative efforts upon closure of significantly deficient investigations reopened as a result of our evaluation.

Subsequent to publishing the Draft Report, we provided the MCIOs a spreadsheet listing of observations and all deficiencies, minor and significant. This allowed them to review the minor deficiency findings and provide mitigating or extenuating information if available. Through a series of conversations and discussions with the MCIOs, we analyzed their responses to the minor deficiencies and made changes to the database and report as appropriate.

Appendix B

This Appendix provides a complete listing of case details, some of which is repetitive of information contained in the report body. Such repetition is intentional to allow the reader to review all data without having to refer between the report and this Appendix to find associated information. The Appendix also contains interesting information related to: use of intoxicants; offense locations; primary offenses involved; other case information including cases with multiple subjects, multiple victims, non-stranger cases; subject data including alcohol involvement, age, military affiliation, rank, punishment information, and sex offender registration requirements; and victim information including age, gender, relationship with subject and cooperation with law enforcement.

Case Details

On request, the MCIOs provided a list of 381 child sexual assault cases, which made up our population. We, in turn, forwarded the list to the DoD OIG QMD. QMD provides statistical computations and detailed analysis tailored to specific projects. We asked QMD to provide a simple random sample of cases using a 90-percent confidence level and a 5-percent precision rate. QMD randomly selected a sample consisting of 163 cases (CID – 79, NCIS – 54, and AFOSI – 30) from the lists provided by the MCIOs for evaluation. We provided each MCIO with a list of the randomly selected cases, which the MCIOs made available to us. Of the 163 cases evaluated, 57 cases were determined to have no investigative deficiencies (reflected in Table B.1.).

We also obtained information such as alcohol use by the subject and victim, their age ranges, pay grade, location where offense occurred, the relationship between the subject/victim.

Case Deficiencies

Table B.1. Cases with No Investigative Deficiencies

Total	CID	NCIS	AFOSI
57	39	13	5

Of the 163 cases evaluated, 106 cases (CID – 40, NCIS – 41, and AFOSI – 25) contained either significant or minor investigative deficiencies. Investigative deficiencies were broken down into six subcategories: interview and post-interview deficiencies, evidence deficiencies, crime scene documentation and processing deficiencies, subject-focused actions, investigative coordination/ notification, and documentation (investigative and administrative). The significance of each deficiency noted depended on the impact the deficiency had on the successful resolution of an investigation. Regardless of the category or total number of deficiencies within an investigation, a case annotated as having a single deficiency in any category was deemed deficient. Table B.2 depicts the cases with investigative deficiencies.

Table B.2. Cases with Investigative Deficiencies
(Includes cases returned to the MCIOs)

Total	CID	NCIS	AFOSI
106	40	41	25

A total of 96 cases had one or more minor deficiencies but were nonetheless determined to have met investigative standards. A "minor deficiency" is a task or investigative step the MCIO did not perform, or performed not in conformity with DoD, Service, and MCIO policies and procedures. A minor deficiency is not likely to affect the outcome or have a negative impact on the investigation.

Examples of minor deficiencies include, but are not limited to the following:

- delays in completing logical investigative steps,

- appropriate medical records were not collected and reviewed,

- victim (or parent or guardian) was not issued a DD Form 2701, "Initial Information for Victims and Witnesses of Crime,"

- routine briefs to the victim (or parent or guardian) about the status of the investigation were not provided, and

- fingerprints, mug photographs, and deoxyribonucleic acid (DNA) of subjects were not obtained.

Table B.2a depicts the breakdown by MCIO of cases.

Table B.2a. Cases with Minor Investigative Deficiencies

Total	CID	NCIS	AFOSI
96	34	38	24

Of the 163 cases evaluated, 10 cases (CID – 6, NCIS – 3, and AFOSI – 1) had significant deficiencies. A "significant deficiency" is one or more deficiencies resulting from a material failure(s) to conform with critical elements of DoD, Service, and MCIO policies and procedures. A significant deficiency indicates a breakdown in practices, programs, and/or policies having actual notable adverse impact on, or had a likelihood of materially affecting, the integrity of the investigation and/or adversely affecting or having a high probability of adversely affecting the outcome of an investigation. If our evaluation identified one or more significant deficiencies, the investigation was returned to the MCIO with an explanation of the significant deficiencies identified and the identification of the practices, programs, and/or policies that were not adhered to.

Examples of significant deficiencies include, but are not limited to the following:

- key evidence was not collected from the crime scene, the victim, or the subject;

- crime scene examinations were not completed, not completed thoroughly, or not completed before the loss of crucial evidence;

- sexual assault forensic examinations were not conducted;

- witness interviews were not thorough or not conducted; and

- subject and victim interviews or reinterviews were not thorough or not conducted.

We returned 10 cases identified as being significantly deficient, along with the documented deficiencies, to the respective MCIOs for consideration of additional investigative activity if appropriate. As a result, 8 cases (CID – 4, NCIS – 3, and AFOSI – 1) or 80 percent were reopened by the MCIOs to conduct additional investigative activity. Table B.2b depicts data regarding cases returned and reopened by the MCIOs.

Table B.2b. Cases with Significant Deficiencies

Cases Returned and Reopened	Total	CID	NCIS	AFOSI
Returned	**10**	6	3	1
Reopened	**8**	4	3	1

Cases Returned to CID. We returned six cases to CID for consideration of our findings. On August 8, 2013, CID agreed to reopen four of the six cases to conduct additional activity. CID declined to pursue additional investigative activity in the two remaining cases because they believed it would not alter the outcome of the case or too much time had elapsed, causing the recommended investigative activity to be impracticable. We agreed with CID's assessment of the two remaining cases.

Cases Returned to NCIS. We returned three cases to NCIS for consideration of our findings. On September 26, 2013, NCIS agreed to reopen the returned cases to conduct additional activity.

Cases Returned to AFOSI. We returned one case to AFOSI for consideration of our findings. On July 11, 2013, AFOSI agreed to reopen the returned case to conduct additional activity.

Table B.3 depicts the total number of investigations with interview and post-interview deficiencies. Tables B.4 through B.6 depict interview deficiencies categorized by subject, victim, and witness interviews in an effort to obtain a higher degree of fidelity.

Table B.3. Cases with Interview and Post-Interview Deficiencies

Total	CID	NCIS	AFOSI
78	26	34	18

Table B.4. Cases with Subject Interview and Post-Interview Deficiencies

Total	CID	NCIS	AFOSI
17	2	7	8

Table B.5. Cases with Victim Interview and Post-Interview Deficiencies

Total	CID	NCIS	AFOSI
55	26	18	11

Table B.6. Cases with Witness Interview and Post-Interview Deficiencies

Total	CID	NCIS	AFOSI
44	8	25	11

Tables B.7 through B.9 depict categories of subject, victim, and witness interview deficiencies.

Table B.7. Categories of Subject Interview and Post-Interview Deficiencies

Deficiency	Total	CID	NCIS	AFOSI
Subject interview was not thorough and did not address all the elements of the offense.	**10**	2	4	4
Investigators did not follow up on logical leads stemming from interviews.	**8**	1	3	4
Subject was not interviewed, and the file was not documented explaining why.	**1**	0	0	1

Note: The disparity in the number of cases with subject interview and post-interview deficiencies and the total number of deficiencies is due to some cases having multiple deficiencies.

We noted various deficiencies, which occurred during the subject interviews of the evaluated investigations. Based on the dynamics involved in subject interviews, we recognize there may have been reasons these logical investigative steps were not conducted. However, the evaluated cases did not contain supporting documentation explaining why the subjects were not interviewed nor did they indicate the reasons that all logical information was not addressed.

Table B.8. Victim Interview and Post-Interview Deficiencies

Deficiency	Total	CID	NCIS	AFOSI
Victim interview was not thorough	**11**	3	5	3
Logical leads stemming from interview were not developed or pursued.	**10**	4	2	4
Information provided by victim was not corroborated.	**2**	1	1	0
Multidisciplinary concept was not used.	**6**	1	3	2
Victim or victim's guardian was not issued a DD Form 2701 (or the issuance was not documented as required).	**36**	18	11	7
Routine/recurring victim briefs were not conducted in accordance with (IAW) MCIO policy, or they were not documented.	**11**	1	10	N/A

Note: The disparity in the number of cases with victim interview and post-interview deficiencies and the total number of deficiencies is due to some cases having multiple deficiencies.

Table B.9. Witness Interview and Post-Interview Deficiencies

Deficiency	Total	CID	NCIS	AFOSI
Witnesses were identified but not interviewed, and the file was not documented to explain why.	37	7	21	9
Canvass interviews were not conducted.	17	4	10	3
Witness interview was not thorough.	2	1	1	0

Note: The disparity in the number of cases with witness interview and post-interview deficiencies and the total number of deficiencies is due to some cases having multiple deficiencies.

Table B.10 depicts the total number of cases that contained evidence deficiencies.

Table B.10. Cases with Evidence Deficiencies

Total	CID	NCIS	AFOSI
25	9	10	6

Table B.11 depicts a breakdown of evidence deficiencies.

Table B.11. Evidence Deficiencies

Investigators did not:	Total	CID	NCIS	AFOSI
Collect all items of clothing and bed linen evidence identified by subject(s), victim(s), or witness(es).	4	1	3	0
Collect sexual assault forensic examination evidence of subject(s) or victim(s).	3	1	0	2
Collect appropriate digital evidence identified by subject(s), victim(s), or witness(es).	13	5	5	3
Collect appropriate DNA sample from subject(s), suspect(s), victim(s), and witness(es) for evidence comparison.	5	1	3	1
Submit appropriate computer and/or cell phone to laboratory for examination.	6	1	3	2

Note: The disparity in the number of cases with evidence deficiencies and the total number of deficiencies is due to some cases having multiple deficiencies.

Table B.12 depicts the total number of cases that contained crime scene documentation and/or processing deficiencies.

Table B.12. Cases with Crime Scene Documentation and/or Processing Deficiencies

Total	CID	NCIS	AFOSI
33	12	13	8

Table B.13 depicts a breakdown of crime scene documentation and processing deficiencies.

Table B.13. Crime Scene Documentation and Processing Deficiencies

Investigators did not:	Total	CID	NCIS	AFOSI
Examine or validate the crime scene.	**23**	6	11	6
Have documented authority to search the scene.	**1**	1	0	0
Photograph the scene.	**2**	0	1	1
Sketch the scene.	**3**	3	N/A	N/A
Collect potential evidence from the scene.	**7**	3	2	2

Note: The disparity in the number of cases with evidence deficiencies and the total number of deficiencies is due to some cases having multiple deficiencies.

Table B.14 depicts a breakdown of subject-focused action deficiencies.

Table B.14. Cases with Subject-Focused Action Deficiencies

Investigators did not:	Total	CID	NCIS	AFOSI
Comply with guidance regarding the release of subject(s)/suspect(s) to unit personnel.	**8**	4	4	0
Conduct criminal history records checks on subject(s).	**4**	2	2	0

Table B.15 depicts a breakdown of specific deficiencies for the area of investigative coordination and administrative documentation.

Table B.15. Cases with Investigative Coordination and Administrative Deficiencies

Deficiency	Total	CID	NCIS	AFOSI
Investigators did not immediately coordinate/notify forensic science consultant.	4	N/A	N/A	4
Required supervisory reviews were not documented.	3	0	3	0
Review/inclusion of other law enforcement agency's report was not documented.	2	0	1	1
Location of offense was not fully identified.	2	0	1	1

Intoxicant Use

We identified the following details regarding intoxicant use (alcohol and/or drug) in the evaluated investigations.

- In 10 of the 163 cases evaluated, the subject was determined to have consumed alcohol and/or an over-the counter drug prior to the commission of the offense.

- In 3 of the 163 cases evaluated, the victim was determined to have consumed alcohol and/or an illicit drug.

- In 1 case, both the victim and the subject ingested alcohol prior to the commission of a sexual assault.

Table B.16 depicts the total number of cases where the subject(s) was or was not under the influence of alcohol and/or drugs. The table also shows, where applicable, the type of intoxicant the subject(s) used.

Table B.16. Cases with Subject Alcohol and/or Drug Use

Intoxicant	Total	CID	NCIS	AFOSI
Alcohol	8	2	2	4
Alcohol and over-the-counter drug	1	0	0	1
Over-the-counter drug	1	1	0	0

Intoxicant	Total	CID	NCIS	AFOSI
Unknown/undetermined*	53	24	16	13
None	67	31	24	12
Not applicable	33	21	12	0

*Alcohol and/or drug use by the subject(s) in 53 investigations could not be determined because the information about such use was not available in the case files.

Table B.17 depicts the total number of cases in which the victim(s) was under the influence of alcohol and/or drugs. In each case in which a victim was reported to have consumed alcohol or drugs, the consumption was voluntary and the victim was between the ages of 14 and 17. The table also shows, where applicable, the type of intoxicant the victim(s) used.

Table B.17. Cases with Voluntary Victim Alcohol and/or Drug Use

Voluntary Alcohol or Drug Use	Total	CID	NCIS	AFOSI
Alcohol	2	2	0	0
Alcohol with illicit drug	1	1	0	0
Unknown/undetermined*	18	9	3	6
None	138	67	48	23
Not applicable	4	0	3	1

*Alcohol and/or drug use by the victim(s) in 18 investigations could not be determined because the information about such use was not available in the case files.

Table B.18 depicts the total number of cases in which both the subject(s) and victim(s) were under the influence of alcohol and/or drugs.

Table B.18. Cases with Alcohol and/or Drug Use by Both Subject and Victim

Total	CID	NCIS	AFOSI
1	1	0	0

Offense Location

The majority of sexual assault incidents (96 of 163 or 59 percent) occurred on a military installation, while 51 of 163 (31 percent) occurred outside of a military installation. Many occurred in a residence/home (112 of 163 or 69 percent).

These numbers indicate the majority of sexual assaults against children occur in an environment familiar to the subject or victim. Tables B.19 and B.20 provide details regarding offense location data.

Table B.19 depicts the number of cases where the crime occurred on or off the installation.

Table B.19. Cases Where the Sexual Assault Occurred On/Off the Installation

Location	Total	CID	NCIS	AFOSI
On installation	97	60	32	5
Off installation	51	14	13	24
Unknown	15	5	9	1

Table B.20 depicts where the sexual assault took place.

Table B.20. Where the Sexual Assault Occurred

Category	Total	CID	NCIS	AFOSI
Barracks/dorm	5	2	3	0
Daycare or child development center	2	2	0	0
Government vehicle	1	0	1	0
Hotel/motel	4	0	1	3
Office/workplace	1	0	0	1
Park/beach	3	2	0	1
Parking lot	3	2	1	0
Prison/brig	1	0	1*	0
Private vehicle	3	3	0	0
Residence/home	112	56	35	21
Retail store	1	0	1	0
School	4	3	1	0
Swimming pool	2	1	1	0
Wooded/open area	4	2	1	1
Unidentified	17	6	8	3

*The subject in this instance was a prison inmate who wrote a letter to a female under the age of 16 in an effort to entice her into committing future sexual acts with him.

Primary Offense

Although several offenses may have been investigated and/or charged, we documented only the primary offense investigated. Table B.21 depicts number of cases by type of offense investigated.

Table B.21. Primary Offense Investigated

Offense	Total	CID	NCIS	AFOSI
Abusive sexual contact with a child	15	3	10	2
Aggravated sexual abuse of a child under 12	12	6	3	3
Aggravated sexual abuse of a child 12 to under 16	9	9	0	0
Aggravated sexual assault of a child under 12	11	4	6	1
Aggravated sexual assault of a child under 12 (attempted)	4	1	1	2
Aggravated sexual assault of a child 12 to under 16	30	15	9	6
Aggravated sexual assault of a child 12 to under 16 (attempted)	2	0	2	0
Aggravated sexual contact with a child under 12	16	4	8	4
Aggravated sexual contact with a child 12 to under 16	17	10	3	4
Indecent liberties with a child	18	6	7	5
Rape of a child under 12	17	14	3	0
Rape of a child under 12 (attempted)	1	0	1	0
Rape of a child 12 to under 16	9	6	0	3
Sodomy of a child under 12	1	1	0	0
Sodomy of a child 12 to under 16	1	0	1	0
Total	**163**	**79**	**54**	**30**

Table B.22 depicts the number of cases that involved multiple subjects.

Table B.22. Cases with Multiple Subjects

Total	CID	NCIS	AFOSI
7	5	0	2

Table B.23 depicts the number of cases that involved multiple victims.

Table B.23. Cases with Multiple Victims

Total	CID	NCIS	AFOSI
27	17	6	4

Table B.24 depicts the number of cases that involved multiple subjects and multiple victims.

Table B.24. Cases with Multiple Subjects and Multiple Victims

Total	CID	NCIS	AFOSI
3	3	0	0

Table B.25 depicts the number of cases in which the victim(s) knew or had a relationship with the subject(s) prior to the sexual assault.

Table B.25. Cases in Which Victim Knew Subject

Total	CID	NCIS	AFOSI
145	68	49	28

Note: At table B.38 is a detailed breakdown of the subject-to-victim relationships.

We identified the following details regarding the subject-to-victim relationship in the evaluated investigations.

- 67 of 163 investigations, the subject(s) was a family member (father, step-father, brother, half-brother, step-brother, brother-in-law, or mother) of the victim(s).

- 91 of 163 investigations, the subject(s) was not a family member of the victim.

- 5 of 163 investigations, no person was listed as a victim; therefore, the relationship information is not applicable.

We noted 7 of 163 cases with multiple subjects and 27 cases with multiple victims. In these instances, the cases identified two or more subjects as perpetrating the offense under investigation, or in the circumstance of the victims, the case listed two or more victims being victimized in an individual investigation. We also noted 33 of the 163 cases had no subject because the cases were either unfounded or there was insufficient evidence to prove or disprove a crime occurred. In five investigations, no victim was identified. In these cases, subjects were attempting to commit crimes with children by communicating with persons they believed to be children. The intended victims were actually law enforcement officials posing as children. As a result, a total of 138 subjects and 201 victims (individuals) were identified.

We noted the following highlights of the 138 subjects in the evaluated investigations.

- Of the 138 subjects, 10 (7 percent) consumed alcohol prior to the commission of a sexual assault.

- The majority of subjects ranged in ages from 18 to 23 (37 of 138 or 27 percent) and 24 to 29 years old (37 of 138 or 27 percent).

- Of the 138 subjects, 18 (13 percent) were juveniles.

Of the 138 subjects, 94 (68 percent) were military personnel. The majority were enlisted members (90 of 138 or 65 percent) with E-4s (24 of 138 or 17 percent) and E-5s (22 of 138 or 16 percent) comprising the largest pool of subjects. Although a limited number of commissioned officers perpetrated child sexual assaults, all of the subjects in the commissioned officers corps (4 out of 138 or 3 percent) were junior officers in the grades of O-1 through O-3 (company-grade officers).

Of the 138 subjects, 68 (49 percent) received no punishment (adverse action taken against them) as a result of the investigation; 2 (1 percent) received nonjudicial punishment; and 38 (28 percent) were convicted by courts-martial or civilian courts. Action against seven (5 percent) subjects was not applicable because they were listed as unknown in the investigations.

The following tables (B.26-B.39) address individual subjects and victims and not the number of cases. Therefore, the numbers noted will exceed the number of cases evaluated. This is due to the number of cases with multiple subjects and victims. There were a total of 138 subjects and 201 victims in the 163 cases we evaluated. These tables are statistical in nature and contain no deficiencies.

Table B.26 depicts the number of subjects that were under the influence of alcohol and/or drugs. The table also shows, where applicable, the type of intoxicant the subject(s) used.

Table B.26. Subjects Alcohol and/or Drug Involvement

Category:	Total	CID	NCIS	AFOSI
Alcohol	9	3	2	4
Alcohol with over-the-counter drug	1	0	0	1
Over-the-counter drug	1	1	0	0
Unknown/undetermined	62	31	18	13
None	65	30	22	13

Table B.27 depicts the age ranges of each subject.

Table B.27. Age Range of Subjects

Category:	Total	CID	NCIS	AFOSI
12-13	3	1	2	0
14-15	9	7	2	0
16-17	6	4	2	0
18-23	37	19	14	4
24-29	37	15	12	10
30-35	25	13	3	9
36-40	9	1	3	5
41-45	2	1	0	1
46-50	1	0	0	1
51-55	1	0	1	0
Over 55	1	0	0	1
Unknown	7	4	3	0

Table B.28 depicts the subject's affiliation.

Table B.28. Subject's Affiliation

Category:	Total	CID	NCIS	AFOSI
Military	94	37	28	29
Civilian	37	24	11	2
Unknown	7	4	3	0

Table B.29 depicts the military subject's pay grade.

Table B.29. Military Subject's Pay Grade

Category:	Total	CID	NCIS	AFOSI
E-1	1	0	1	0
E-2	5	2	3	0
E-3	16	5	7	4
E-4	24	15	6	3
Junior Enlisted	**46**	**22**	**17**	**7**
E-5	22	8	6	8
E-6	11	3	3	5
NCO	**33**	**11**	**9**	**13**
E-7	8	3	1	4
E-8	3	1	1	1
E-9	0	0	0	0
Senior NCO	**11**	**4**	**2**	**5**
Total Enlisted	**90**	**37**	**28**	**25**
Warrant Grade	**0**	**0**	**0**	**0**
O-1	1	0	0	1
O-2	0	0	0	0
O-3	3	0	0	3
Company Grade	**4**	**0**	**0**	**4**
Field Grade	**0**	**0**	**0**	**0**
Flag Officer	**0**	**0**	**0**	**0**
Total Officer	**4**	**0**	**0**	**4**
Military Total	**94**	**37**	**28**	**29**

Table B.30 depicts the action that was taken on the subjects of the investigations.

Table B.30. Action Taken Against Subjects

Category:	Total	CID	NCIS	AFOSI
Convicted by trial for sexual assault offenses	38	14	14	10
Convicted by trial for lesser non sexual assault offenses	7	2	3	2
Acquitted by trial	2	0	1	1
Discharged from service in lieu of trial	5	5	0	0
Nonjudicial (Article 15)	1	0	0	1
Nonjudicial and discharged	1	1	0	0
Reprimand/counseling	4	1	0	3
Unknown[1]	5	1	2	2
No action taken[2]	68	37	19	12
Not applicable (unknown subjects)	7	4	3	0
Totals	**138**	**65**	**42**	**31**

[1] For five investigations that the MCIOs categorized as being closed, no disciplinary action information was available.

[2] It is the decision of the subject's action commander or civilian prosecutor to determine if there is sufficient evidence to warrant the taking of punitive action against the subject. Additional information about the cases with no action taken is provided at tables B.33 and B.34.

Table B.31 depicts the court directed action that was taken against military subjects convicted of sexual assault offenses. Of the 38 subjects convicted by trial for sexual offenses, 31 were active duty military. Of the 31 military subjects convicted, 26 were tried by courts-martial and 5 were tried by civilian courts. The majority of the convicted military subjects received multiple types of punishment; therefore, cumulative totals will exceed the total number of convicted military subjects.

Table B.31. Action Taken Against Convicted Military Subjects

Category:	Total	CID	NCIS	AFOSI
Confinement	27	10	10	7
Fines and forfeitures	19	8	6	5
Reduction in rank	20	9	7	4
Dishonorable discharge	11	5	3	3
Bad conduct discharge	10	4	5	1

Table B.32 depicts the court-directed action that was taken against civilian subjects convicted of sexual assault offenses. Of the 38 subjects convicted by trial for sexual offenses, 7 were civilians tried by civilian courts. The majority of the convicted civilians received multiple types of punishment; therefore, cumulative totals will exceed the total number of convicted civilian subjects.

Table B.32. Action Taken Against Convicted Civilian Subjects

Category:	Total	CID	NCIS	AFOSI
Confinement	6	3	2	1
Parole after confinement	2	2	0	0
Probation (no confinement)	1	0	1	0
Fines and forfeitures	1	1	0	0

Table B.33 depicts the numbers of military and civilian subjects in which no action was taken against them.

Table B.33. No Action Taken Against Military and Civilian Subjects

Category:	Total	CID	NCIS	AFOSI
Military	42	17	13	12
Civilian	26	20	6	0
Totals	**68**	**37**	**19**	**12**

Table B.34 depicts the status of the cases at the time of closure when no action was taken against the subjects.

Table B.34. Case Status at Closure When No Action Taken Against Subjects

Category:	Total	CID	NCIS	AFOSI
Insufficient evidence	7	4	3	0
Unresolved/unfounded	8	7	0	1
Resolved/solved*	53	26	16	11
Totals	**68**	**37**	**19**	**12**

*Cases that are closed as resolved/solved are often closed indicating there is probable cause to believe a subject committed the investigated crime. It is the decision of the subject's action commander or a civilian prosecutor to determine if there is sufficient evidence to warrant the taking of punitive action against the subject.

Table B.35 depicts the number of subjects ordered to register as sex offenders as a result of their conviction.

Table B.35. Subjects Ordered to Register as Sex Offenders

Category:	Total	CID	NCIS	AFOSI
Ordered to register	**29**	8	11	10

We noted the following highlights of the 201 victims in the evaluated investigations.

- The majority of victims, 63 of 201 (31 percent), ranged in age from 14 to 15. The second largest group of victims (51 or 25 percent), were between 2 and 5 years old.

- Of the 201 victims, 166 (83 percent) were female and 35 (17 percent) were male.

- Unlike in cases of sexual assaults against adult victims, we found alcohol and drug use to be rare in cases of sexual assaults against child victims. Of the 201 victims identified in this project, 3 victims consumed alcohol and 1 consumed alcohol with an illicit drug. These 4 victims ranged in age from 14 to 17. All four victims voluntarily consumed the intoxicating substance(s).

Table B.36 depicts the age ranges of each victim. Although there were 201 victims listed in the cases we evaluated, 5 were victimized while they were in 2 different age groups and 4 were victimized while they were in 3 different age groups. Five victims were in the age range category of 16 to 17. Three of these victims were involved in cases with other victims who were children, one was victimized while also in the age group category of 14 to 15, and one was included in this project because the state where the crime occurred specified a child as being a person under the age of 17.

Table B.36. Age Range of Victims

Category:	Total	CID	NCIS	AFOSI
Under 2	**2**	1	1	0
2-5	**51**	31	13	7
6-9	**46**	28	12	6
10-11	**22**	12	8	2
12-13	**25**	16	4	5
14-15	**63**	29	19	15
16-17	**5**	1	1	3

Table B.37 depicts the gender of the victims.

Table B.37. Victim's Gender

Category:	Total	CID	NCIS	AFOSI
Male	35	18	9	8
Female	166	90	48	28

Table B.38 depicts the subject-to-victim relationship type.

Table B.38. Subject-to-Victim Relationship Type

Category:	Total	CID	NCIS	AFOSI
Boyfriend	3	1	2	0
Boyfriend of mother	3	1	2	0
Brother	3	2	1	0
Brother (half, in-law, step)	14	5	7	2
Caregiver	2	1	1	0
Classmate	3	3	0	0
Clergy	1	0	0	1
Cousin	3	1	1	1
Father	43	24	6	13
Father (step)	33	26	2	5
Friend/acquaintance of victim	56	23	20	13
Friend/acquaintance of a family member of victim	17	9	8	0
Grandfather	2	0	2	0
Girlfriend of a relative	1	0	0	1
Mother	1	0	1	0
Stranger	3	1	2	0
Teacher	1	1	0	0
Uncle	1	0	1	0
No relationship or not applicable	11	10	1	0

Table B.39 depicts the number of victims that were cooperative during the investigation.

Table B.39. Victim Cooperation

Category:	Total	CID	NCIS	AFOSI
Yes	187	99	55	33
No	14	9	2	3

See Appendix D for a complete listing of all tables provided.

Appendix C

Memorandum of Results

October 22, 2013

Memorandum of Results

To: ████████████████, Violent Crime Division,
Oversight Directorate, Investigative Policy and Oversight

From: ██████████████████████, QMD/AUDIT

Thru: ██████████████████████, QMD/AUDIT

Subject: QMD Support in Review of Department of Defense Child Sexual Assault Review Project No. 2013C002.

Objective. The objective of the project is to evaluate the adequacy of child sexual assault investigations, specifically to determine whether the Military Criminal Investigative Organizations (MCIOs) investigative procedures comply with DoD and Military Service guidance, and whether the MCIOs adequately investigated the child sexual assaults as required by the standards. The evaluation scope will consider child sexual assault investigations with cases closed in the calendar year 2012.

Population. The population for the three MCIOs for cases closed for child sexual assaults during the calendar year 2012 is tabulated below:

	MCIOs	Number of Closed Cases
1.	CID	188
2.	NCIS	128
3.	AFOSI	65
	Total	*381*

Measures. The attribute measure was the number of deficiencies in the child sexual assault cases during the investigation process.

Parameters. We designed the sample at 90% confidence level and 5% precision.

Methodology. We developed Simple Random Sample (SRS) plan for each MCIO, and randomly selected samples without replacement for each organization. A summary table of the population size, sample size, and the number of cases reviewed is provided below:

Memorandum of Results (cont'd)

	MCIOs	Population Size	Sample Size	Cases Reviewed
1.	CID	188	79	79
2.	NCIS	128	54	54
3.	AFOSI	65	30	30
	Total	*381*	*163*	*163*

The team reviewed each of the 163 sample cases, and provided to QMD the deficiencies or other related problems found in each sample case. After review and analysis of the sample results, we computed statistical projections over the three MCIOs by using the sample results and the applicable SRS formulae. We aggregated the projections for the three MCIOs to represent DoD projections by using stratified sample formulae with MCIOs as the three strata. The projections are included in the attached spreadsheet. Each line in the spreadsheet provides the relevant information, i.e., population size, sample size, number of cases with errors, statistically projected number of cases (and percentages) with errors as the lower bound, the point estimate, and the upper bound.

An illustration of the interpretation of the statistical results for the first line in the attachment for "Adequate Cases" would be: CID with a population of 188 cases and a sample of 79 cases has 73 adequate cases in the sample, and we are 90% confident that the projected number of adequate cases in the population is between 165 and 182, and the point estimate is 174; we are 90% confident that the rate of the number of cases excluded is between 88.0% and 96.8%, and the point estimate is 92.4%. All the other lines in the spreadsheet can also be interpreted in the same way.

Attachment: Spreadsheet

Appendix D

Table Listing

Table Listing (cont'd)

Appendix E

Independent Review

INSPECTOR GENERAL
DEPARTMENT OF DEFENSE
4800 MARK CENTER DRIVE
ALEXANDRIA, VIRGINIA 22350-1500

July 31, 2014

MEMORANDUM FOR DEPUTY INSPECTOR GENERAL FOR POLICY AND OVERSIGHT

SUBJECT: Limited Scope Assessment of Investigative Policy and Oversight (IPO), Violent Crime Division's (VCD) final report, "Evaluation of Military Criminal Investigative Organizations' Child Sexual Assault Investigations"

Personnel within my office performed a limited scope assessment of the subject IPO VCD final report to verify that IPO VCD appropriately addressed management comments and made appropriate adjustments in assuring that the report is factually accurate.

The IPO VCD final report as currently written satisfies the Quality Standards for Inspection and Evaluation (Blue Book) for evidence and reporting. In performing this assessment we in limited instances deferred to the professional judgment of IPO VCD.

If you have any questions regarding this memorandum, please contact me at (703) 604-8877 or by email at Carolyn.Davis@dodig.mil.

Carolyn R. Davis
Assistant Inspector General
Audit Policy and Oversight

Management Comments

CID Comments

DEPARTMENT OF THE ARMY
U. S. ARMY CRIMINAL INVESTIGATION COMMAND
27130 TELEGRAPH ROAD
QUANTICO, VA 22134

REPLY TO
ATTENTION OF

CIOP-ZC

MAR 1 0 2014

Memorandum For Inspector General, Department of Defense, Attn: Mr. Randolph Stone, 4800 Mark Center Drive, Alexandria, VA 22350-1500

Subject: Military Criminal Investigative Organizations Investigated Most Child Sexual Assaults in Compliance with Policy and Guidance (Project #2013C002)

1. Thank you for the opportunity to review and comment on this third in a recent series of Department of Defense Inspector General (DoDIG) reports on sexual assault investigations. As stated in comments provided concerning the previous reports, I remain concerned that the DoDIG inspection process fails to adhere to the standards as established by the Council of the Inspectors General on Integrity and Efficiency (CIGIE). And again, I find that it is fatally flawed in many areas.

2. The basic tenet of IG inspections as outlined by the CIGIE is that they be credible and useful for agency managers, policy makers and others. This DoDIG review failed to be credible or useful as the findings were not adequately supported.

   a. First and foremost, the title of the report does not accurately reflect the findings of the inspection. The use of the word "most" implies something above 51%, but fails to recognize the MCIOs achieved a 93% compliance rate in their investigations of child sexual abuse. Recommend the title be changed to read "Review of Military Criminal Investigative Organizations' Compliance with Policy and Guidance in the Investigation of Child Sexual Assaults."

   b. The review found 6 of 79 Army cases with significant deficiencies. Significant deficiencies were defined as those errors that could have an adverse impact on, or materially affect, the outcome of the investigation. The DoDIG review also found 42 cases with minor deficiencies. Minor deficiencies were defined as those errors that were not likely to affect the outcome of the investigation or have a negative impact on the investigation. The DoDIG inspection team inexplicably combined the significant and minor deficiencies together, then focused a major portion of the report discussing them as if they were equally important. Recommend the report delineate the significant from the insignificant.

   c. Initially, the DoDIG inspection team refused to share the source of the alleged minor deficiencies with the MCIOs. When the MCIOs voiced concerns with their inability to verify that any of the alleged minor deficiencies were factual, the DoDIG reversed its stand and provided the alleged minor deficiencies to the MCIOs. Unfortunately, after removing some of the contested minor deficiencies when shown by

CID Comments (cont'd)

CIOP-ZC
SUBJECT: Military Criminal Investigative Organizations Investigated Most Child Sexual
Assaults in Compliance with Policy and Guidance (Project #2013C002)

the MCIOs to be factually incorrect, the DoDIG team added more minor deficiencies that
had not been included in the original review. The lack of forthrightness and
transparency by the DoDIG is concerning. Recommend the DoDIG review its
inspection processes and ensure it complies with recognized IG standards for
documenting findings.

    d. In discussing alleged deficiencies in the interviews and post-interviews of victims
(Table 6), the DoDIG combined administrative deficiencies with investigative
deficiencies. While the issuance of a DD Form 2701 to the victim (or the victim's
parent/guardian) and the routine/recurring briefings to the victim (or the victim's
parent/guardian) are critical considerations to ensure the victim is adequately informed
about the various agencies and points of contact available to assist the victim with the
aftermath of an assault and status of the investigation, those two issues do not affect
the thoroughness or outcome of the investigation. Recommend those two issues be
removed from Table 6 and the ensuing discussion and be moved to Table 11, which
addresses administrative deficiencies in investigations.

3. Reference the recommendations made in the report.

    a. Contrary to the DoDIG inference in the report's first recommendation that we do
not emphasize thorough completion of all child sexual assault investigations; we will
"continue to" emphasize thorough investigations, as indicative of this MCIO's 92%
compliance rate.

    b. The second recommendation incorrectly assesses the findings. The DoDIG
review cannot say that DD Forms 2701 were not issued to the victims, it can only say
that the issuance was not documented in a case file. Rather than recommending the
MCIOs "implement measures to improve compliance with the issuing" of the DD Form
2701, the recommendation should be re-worded to "implement measures to either
improve the issuing of the DD Forms 2701 or the documentation of such issuances in
case files."

    c. The third recommendation addresses interviews and recommends the MCIOs
"continue to place increased emphasis on interview thoroughness." While it is noted
that less than 7% of all the significant and minor deficiencies had alleged interview
thoroughness deficiencies, CID concurs that the thoroughness of interviews will
continue to be emphasized within the organization.

    d. The fourth recommendation addresses the collection of evidence and
recommends that CID "evaluate existing policies and enhance its guidance regarding

2

CID Comments (cont'd)

CIOP-ZC
SUBJECT: Military Criminal Investigative Organizations Investigated Most Child Sexual Assaults in Compliance with Policy and Guidance (Project #2013C002)

the collection of digital evidence" pertaining to suspects and victims. While the DoDIG review noted that CID policy mandates the preservation and collection of digital evidence during the course of criminal investigations, it did not identify any failure to collect digital evidence. Absent a finding of fault, a more appropriate recommendation would be that "CID continue to evaluate its existing policies to determine if some enhancements may be necessary."

4. We stand ready and willing to assist the DoDIG in any efforts it may undertake to improve the quality of criminal investigations undertaken by CID. We remain committed to ensuring the best possible support to our Army Soldiers, Civilians and Families.

5. The point of contact is ███████████, 571-305-4302 or email
████████████

DAVID E. QUANTOCK
Major General, USA
Commanding

3

NCIS Comments

DEPARTMENT OF THE NAVY
HEADQUARTERS
NAVAL CRIMINAL INVESTIGATIVE SERVICE
27130 TELEGRAPH ROAD
QUANTICO VA 22134-2253

March 14, 2014

MEMORANDUM FOR DEPUTY INSPECTIOR GENERAL, INSPECTOR GENERAL
DEPARTMENT OF DEFENSE

SUBJECT: Military Criminal Investigative Organizations Investigated Most Child Sexual
Assaults in Compliance with Policy and Guidance (Project No. 2013C002)
Naval Criminal Investigative Service Response

The Naval Criminal Investigative Service (NCIS) reviewed the draft report on the
Military Criminal Investigative Organizations Investigated Most Child Sexual Assaults in
Compliance with Policy and Guidance (Project No. 2013C002). I have provided the
below information in response to the report.

The DoD IG evaluated investigations of sexual assaults of children completed in
2012 to determine whether the Military Criminal Investigative Organizations (MCIO)
completed investigations as required by DoD, Military Service, and MCIO guidance. As
a result of their evaluation, the DoD IG identified six recommendations requiring NCIS
comment. Specifically, the DoD IG recommended: (1) NCIS emphasize thorough
completion of all child sexual assault investigations, (2) NCIS implement measures to
improve compliance with issuing of DD Form 2701, "Initial Information for Victims and
Witnesses of Crime," (3) NCIS continue to place increased emphasis on interview
thoroughness through continued training, supervision and policy improvements, (4) NCIS
enhance guidance and increase training on the critical role clothing and digital evidence
have in child sexual assault investigations, (5) NCIS evaluate and enhance existing
policies regarding the collection of digital evidence and other electronic media used by
subjects and victims, (6) NCIS improve guidance and enhance supervision regarding the
response to crime scenes.

In response: (1) NCIS has and will continue to emphasize thorough completion of
all child sexual assault investigations as required by DoD, Service, and NCIS regulatory
guidance; and (2) NCIS is currently revising policy regarding child sexual assault
investigations. Included in the revisions is specific guidance for the delivery of the DD
Form 2701 to appropriate family members or guardians of child victims. In regard to
Recommendation (3), NCIS has and will continue to emphasize interview thoroughness
and the pursuit of logical leads. In response to Recommendations (4) through (6), NCIS
is currently revising policy regarding child sexual assault investigations. Included in the
revisions is specific guidance for the identification and collection of evidence; to include,

NCIS Comments (cont'd)

clothing, digital, and electronic storage evidence. Referenced policy revisions will include an emphasis on crime scene response.

In addition to the provided responses to the specific DoD IG recommendations, it is important to note NCIS' Advanced Family and Sexual Violence Training Program (AFSVTP). The NCIS AFSVTP is an NCIS created, advanced course designed to provide NCIS investigators advanced and continuing education relevant to child abuse and domestic violence investigations. Initially, the AFSVTP included adult sexual assault investigations training but the two week course has been revised to focus strictly on child abuse and domestic violence investigations. Within the AFSVTP, NCIS investigators receive training from nationally recognized subject matter experts as well as DoD experts. In response to this captioned DoD IG report and evolving requirements identified within the DoD Special Victim Capability program, NCIS has scheduled a curriculum review for the AFSVTP for April 2014. During the curriculum review, the DoD IG recommendations will be addressed and included in future AFSVTP courses. Further, NCIS will use results of the AFSVTP curriculum review for inclusion in current NCIS basic training platforms.

In conclusion, NCIS is currently updating policy and training to reflect congressional and DoD IG mandates pertaining to child sexual assault investigations. The Director, Naval Criminal Investigative Service, will ensure the evaluation of child sexual assault investigations continue in an effort to improve the timeliness and thoroughness of investigations and confirm they align with guiding policies and procedures.

Executive Assistant Director (Acting)
Criminal Investigations Directorate

AFOSI Comments

DEPARTMENT OF THE AIR FORCE

AIR FORCE OFFICE OF SPECIAL INVESTIGATIONS

Quantico Virginia

20 February 2014

MEMORANDUM FOR IG, DoD, ATTN: Deputy IG for Policy and Oversight

FROM: HQ AFOSI/XR
27130 Telegraph Road
Quantico, VA 22134

SUBJECT: AFOSI Response to DoDIG Report No. 2013C002 "Military Criminal Investigative Organizations Investigated Most Child Sexual Assaults in Compliance With Policy and Guidance"

1. This memorandum is the Air Force Office of Special Investigations (AFOSI) response to the recommendations contained in draft DoDIG Report No. 2013C002, pertaining to the *Military Criminal Investigative Organizations Investigated Most Child Sexual Assaults in Compliance With Policy and Guidance*. The report requests AFOSI management comments pertaining to five (# 1, 2, 3, 4a and 4c) of the seven total recommendations and sub-recommendations.

2. Pertaining to Recommendation 1, **Adequacy of Investigations**, "We recommend the Director and Commands of Military Criminal Investigative Organizations emphasize thorough completion of all child sexual assault investigations to ensure all investigations are completed as required by DoD, Service, and command regulatory guidance."

    AFOSI Comment: Concur, with comment.

    AFOSI will re-emphasize to its field personnel the importance of thoroughly investigating and reporting findings in all AFOSI investigations. AFOSI is committed to providing high quality investigative products to Air Force decision makers. As part of this re-emphasis, a summary of the valid deficiencies identified in your assessment will also be provided to staff personnel at the USAF Special Investigations Academy (USAFSIA) to help them further highlight during training the importance of conducting thorough, complete investigations.

3. Pertaining to Recommendation 2, **Initial Information for Victims and Witnesses of Crime**, "We recommend the Director and Commanders of Military Criminal Investigative Organizations implement measures to improve compliance with the issuing of DD Form 2701, "Initial Information for Victims and Witnesses of Crime," to the victims or the victim's appropriate family member or guardian."

    AFOSI Comment: Concur, with comment.

    Current AFOSI policy and training sufficiently address the requirement to issue a DD Form 2701. AFOSI agrees more emphasis needs to be given to ensure agents enter appropriate documentation into investigative management systems and case files when a DD Form 2701 is issued. Of note, AFOSI staff assessed data provided by the DoDIG staff related to the specific instance where a DD Form 2701 was not issued. AFOSI found 15 instances; however, Table 6, on page 9 of the draft report, shows 12 deficiencies. AFOSI concurs with 11 of the deficiencies. In a few instances, local law enforcement officials, not AFOSI personnel, interfaced with the respective victim or witness. For your consideration, AFOSI is providing a listing, separate from this memorandum, pertaining to the assessment of the 15 deficiencies.

AFOSI Comments (cont'd)

2

4. Pertaining to Recommendation 3, **Interviews**. "We recommend the Director and Commanders of Military Criminal Investigative Organizations continue to place increased emphasis on interview thoroughness, to include the pursuit of logical leads identified during the interview, through continued training, supervision, and policy improvements."

AFOSI Comment: Concur, with comment.

Interviews are some of the most important and probative investigative activities conducted by investigators. As such, it is essential interviews are thoroughly conducted and logical follow-up leads pursued. In 2013, AFOSI increased its use of the Cognitive Interview technique for victims and key witness interviews. Extensive research into the Cognitive Interview technique shows it results in an increase in both the quantity and quality of information obtained from interviewees. AFOSI continues to emphasis and train the Cognitive Interview technique during basic and advanced training.

AFOSI reviewed the deficiencies identified by DoDIG reviewers pertaining to interviews and does not agree with the judgment that some of these interviews were deficient. For example, in two of the five instances where the victim interview was deemed "...not thorough", per Table 6, page 9, AFOSI investigators did not conduct the interviews in question; investigators from another agency conducted these interviews. In two other interviews where AFOSI investigators conducted the interviews, HQ AFOSI staff case reviewers assess the interviews were thoroughly conducted. In addition, in both of these instances, the interviews were audio and video recorded, as is AFOSI policy when conducting child interviews. It is not known if DoDIG reviewers reviewed the recorded interviews or formed their opinions based only on reviews of the narrative write-ups in the respective reports of investigation. It should also be noted assessing thoroughness in child forensic interviews is not the same as adult interviews, especially for child victims of sexual abuse. Child victims, either due to their developmental level or due to concerns associated with sharing information about their abuse, may not be as forthcoming in providing information as adult interviewees. AFOSI does concur with one of the five deficiencies identified by DoDIG reviewers. For your consideration, AFOSI is providing a listing, separate from this memorandum, pertaining to its assessment of all the interview deficiencies identified in your report.

5. Pertaining to Recommendation 4a, **Collection of Evidence**, "We recommend the Director and Commanders of Military Criminal Investigative Organizations enhance guidance and increase training to highlight the critical role clothing and digital evidence has in child sexual assault investigations and subsequent prosecutions."

AFOSI Comment: Concur, with comment.

AFOSI is currently revising AFOSIMAN 71-124, Crime Scene Manual, last published in 2003. The revision will include revised guidance pertaining to the collection of physical, biological and digital evidence. Guidance added to AFOSIMAN 71-124 will better assist decision making pertaining to evidence recognition and collection, i.e. clothing items. In addition, extensive instruction is provided in AFOSI basic and advanced investigator training courses on the proper recognition, collection and preservation of evidence. In an effort to re-emphasize the critical role of evidence, AFOSI will summarize the valid concerns identified in your assessment and provide this information to USAFSIA to ensure appropriate emphasis on the importance of evidence recognition and collection.

████████████

AFOSI Comments (cont'd)

3

However, AFOSI does not agree with DoDIG findings in some instances. For example, in Table 8, page 10-11, three deficiencies are cited pertaining to "Submit appropriate computer and/or cell phone to laboratory examination." AFOSI does not agree with two of the three deficiencies. In one case, the local police were lead investigative agency and were responsible for actions taken in the investigation. In another instance, there was nothing in the case facts or circumstances indicating there was evidence on the devices and, therefore, there was no supporting legal basis for obtaining the necessary probable cause to obtain search authority to seize the items.

AFOSI also feels this assessment conveys AFOSI policy should embrace protocols that do not allow for field judgments and decisions based on the many variables involved in assessing the potential probative value of evidence. Facts and circumstances of reported offenses vary greatly and directly factor in the probative value of evidence; to include time elapsed from incident to reporting to law enforcement and consensual acts that negate physical analysis of items. In addition, case circumstances and legal limitations may prevent investigators from obtaining the necessary authority to search for and seize evidence, even when such evidence is assessed by investigators to be potentially valuable in a case.

Certainly, general protocols pertaining to evidence are needed and, when in doubt, investigators should attempt to collect clothing or any other evidence deemed to be of possible value to the investigation. However, it is not reasonable or practical to seize all items and send all seized items for laboratory analysis. Instead, AFOSI employs a cadre of forensic science specialists who, by AFOSI policy, are to be consulted in every violent crime case. AFOSI forensic specialists work with case agents to assess the probative value, and perishability concerns of potential items of evidence. AFOSI forensic specialists also frequently consult with crime laboratory personnel in assessing the potential value of specific items. As noted, AFOSI disagrees with the basis for several of the discrepancies pertaining to evidence that are identified in the report. For your consideration, AFOSI is providing a listing, separate from this memorandum, pertaining to its assessment of evidence discrepancies pertaining to AFOSI cases.

6. Pertaining to Recommendation 4c, **Collection of Evidence.** "We recommend the Commander, Air Force Office of Special Investigations, implement measures to improve compliance with existing policies regarding the collection of computers and other digital media."

AFOSI Comment: Concur, with comment.

In an effort to emphasize the critical role of digital evidence, AFOSI will summarize the valid concerns identified in your assessment and provide this information to USAFSIA to ensure appropriate emphasis during training on the importance of evidence recognition and collection. AFOSI currently employs a team of case quality reviewers at HQ AFOSI to assess the sufficiency of AFOSI investigations. HQ case reviewers are aware of the concerns found during your assessment and will provide greater oversight to correcting the deficiencies identified.

However, it is not clear based on the information in the report what the specific basis is for this recommendation, pertaining only to AFOSI to, "...improve compliance with existing policies regarding the collection of computers and other digital media." In Table 8, Evidence Deficiencies, in page 10-11, only two discrepancies were noted for, "Collect appropriate digital evidence..." and three discrepancies noted for, "Submit appropriate computer and/or cell phone to laboratory..." AFOSI's discrepancies for this issue do not seem to be greatly different than those for CID and NCIS. No mention is made about concerns specific to AFOSI pertaining to digital evidence in the "Collection of Evidence" summary following Table 8. No specific

AFOSI Comments (cont'd)

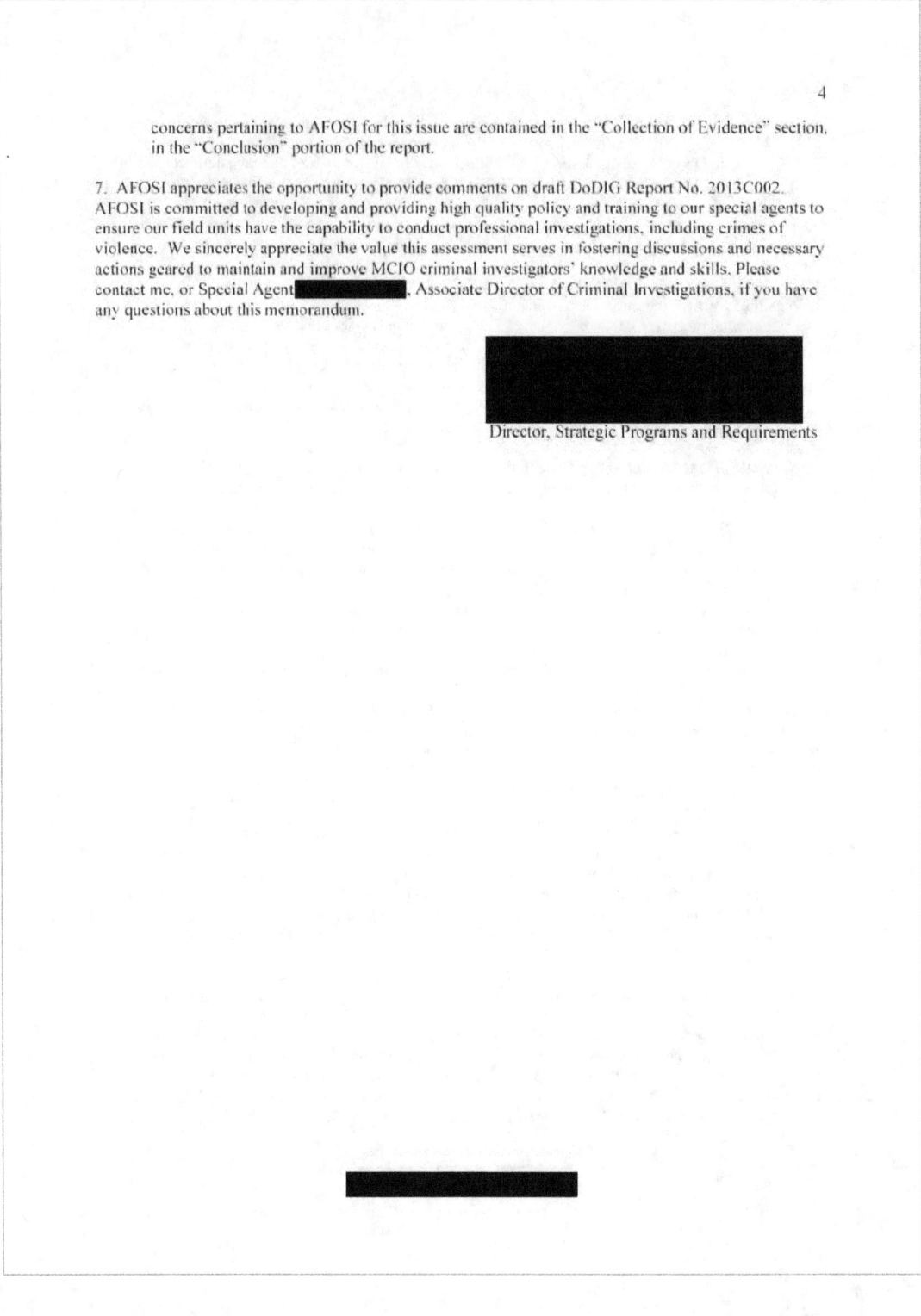

4

concerns pertaining to AFOSI for this issue are contained in the "Collection of Evidence" section, in the "Conclusion" portion of the report.

7. AFOSI appreciates the opportunity to provide comments on draft DoDIG Report No. 2013C002. AFOSI is committed to developing and providing high quality policy and training to our special agents to ensure our field units have the capability to conduct professional investigations, including crimes of violence. We sincerely appreciate the value this assessment serves in fostering discussions and necessary actions geared to maintain and improve MCIO criminal investigators' knowledge and skills. Please contact me, or Special Agent ███████████, Associate Director of Criminal Investigations, if you have any questions about this memorandum.

Director, Strategic Programs and Requirements

Acronyms and Abbreviations

AFI	Air Force Instruction
AFOSI	Air Force Office of Special Investigations
AFOSIH	Air Force Office of Special Investigations Handbook
AFOSIMAN	Air Force Office of Special Investigations Manual
AFPD	Air Force Policy Directive
AFSVTP	Advanced Family and Sexual Violence Training Program
AR	Army Regulation
CID	U.S. Army Criminal Investigations Command
DoDD	Department of Defense Directive
DoDI	Department of Defense Instruction
DoD IG	Department of Defense Inspector General
DNA	Deoxyribonucleic Acid
FAP	Family Advocacy Program
MCIO	Military Criminal Investigative Organization
NCIS	Naval Criminal Investigative Service
OPNAVINST	Department of the Navy Chief of Naval Operations Instruction
QMD	Quantitative Methods Division
SECNAVINST	Secretary of the Navy Instruction
UCMJ	Uniform Code of Military Justice

www.ingramcontent.com/pod-product-compliance
Lightning Source LLC
Chambersburg PA
CBHW081415280526
45788CB00009B/3113